JOHN HERRINGTON

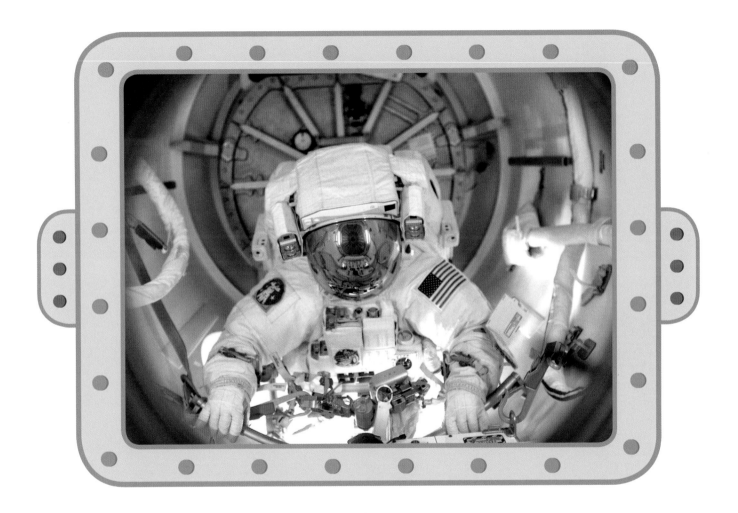

MISSION TO
SPACE

ISBN: 978-1-935684-47-3

Photos courtesy of NASA/JPL-Caltech
Design: Corey Fetters

White Dog Press
c/o Chickasaw Press
PO Box 1548
Ada, Oklahoma 74821

www.chickasawpress.com

I dedicate this book to my dad,
for making the world of flight
possible for a young, adventurous boy.

When I was a little boy, I liked to shoot rockets with my dad and my older brother. Ten, nine, eight...

...seven, six, five, four, three, two, one. Liftoff of the space shuttle Endeavour!

I am Commander John B. Herrington and I am Chickasaw.

Flying in space takes a
lot of training.

I trained in a virtual reality laboratory.

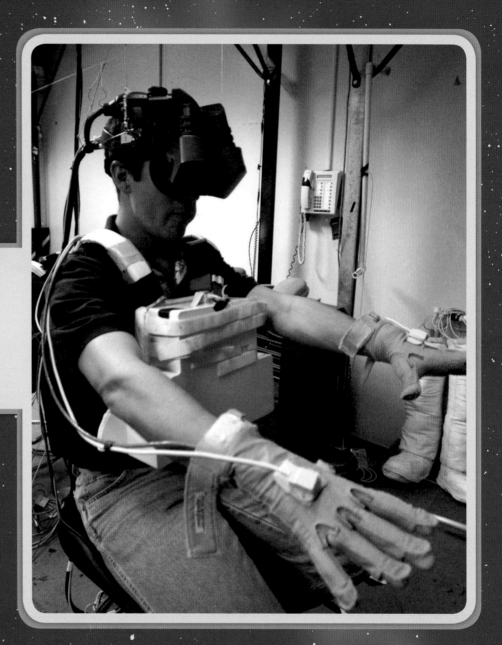

I trained in a pool called the Neutral Buoyancy Laboratory.

It takes a lot of hard work to do something well.

Soon I was ready to fly to the International Space Station with my fellow astronauts.

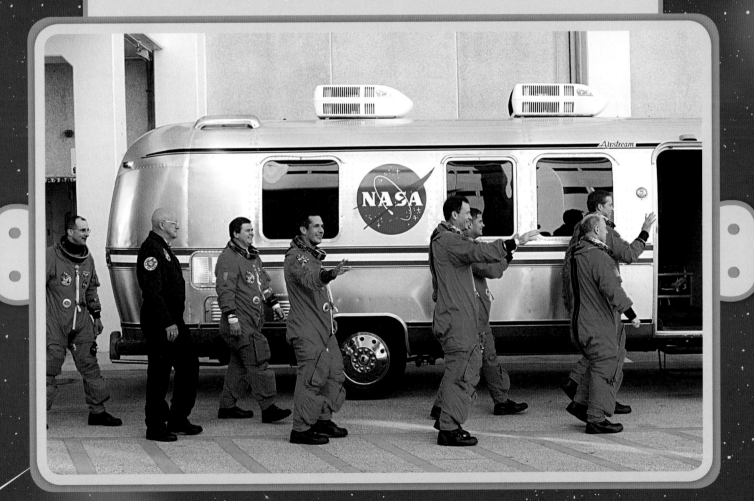

While we waited in the shuttle, there was a very important celebration happening in the Rocket Garden at Kennedy Space Center.

Chickasaw Nation Governor Bill Anoatubby and Lt. Governor Jefferson Keel presented a Chickasaw blanket to NASA.

People came from miles away to sing, dance, and celebrate.

The rockets ignite with a great shudder, and we blast off into orbit around Earth.

The International Space Station
will be our home for the
next two weeks.

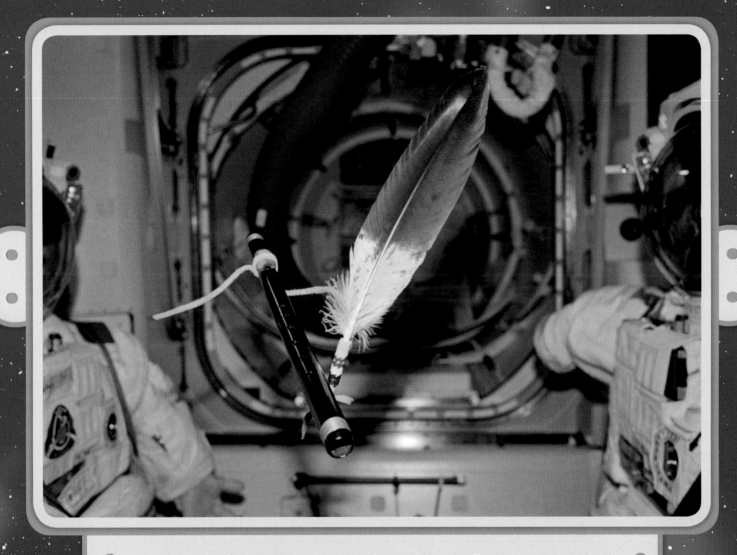

Look! My eagle feather and flute float in space.

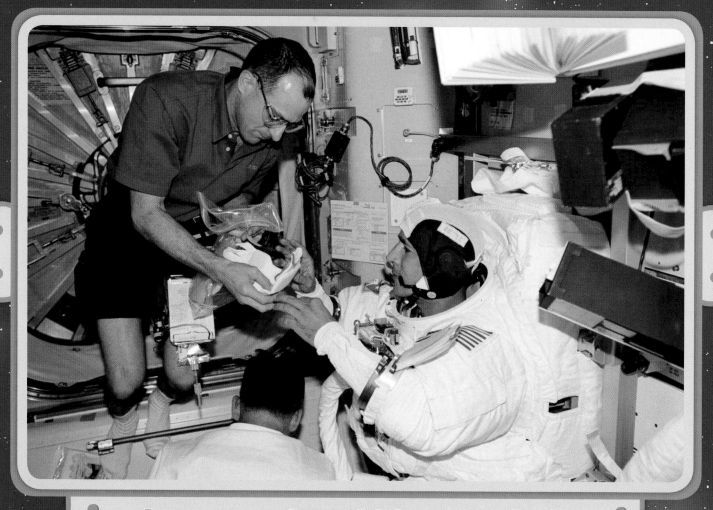

Astronaut Donald R. Pettit helps me with my EMU (Extravehicular Mobility Unit) suit.

Now it is time to spacewalk. Am I upside down or right side up?

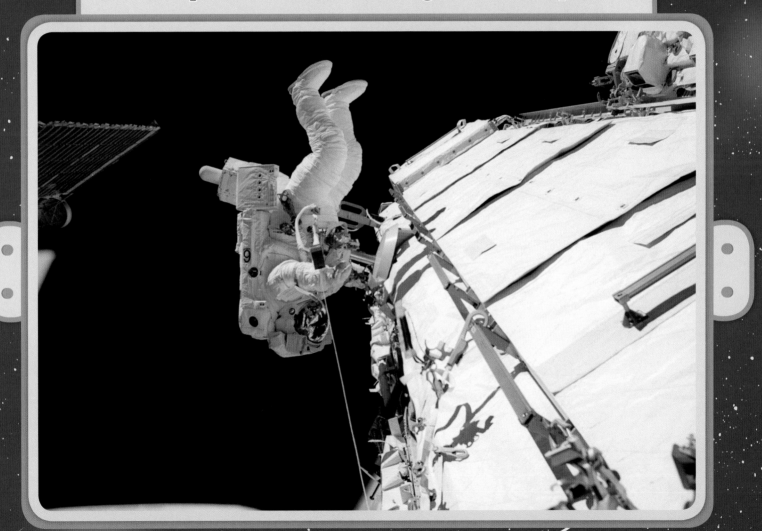

We are 220 miles above Earth. Our helmets, suits, and gloves protect us from the extreme cold and heat.

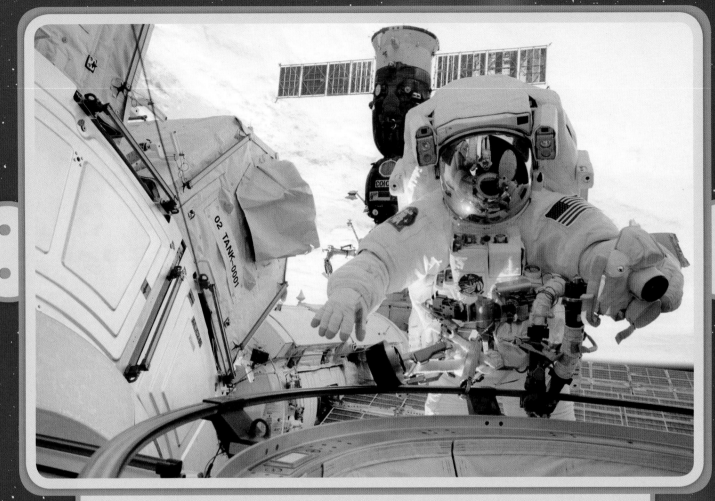

An astronaut's helmet has a special visor. It protects our eyes from the bright light of the sun.

Mission accomplished! We
have successfully landed
back on Earth.

LANGUAGE

The Chickasaw language is an important part of our culture. It's part of what makes us uniquely Chickasaw. Like all languages, it grows and changes as the world around us changes. Often new words are needed to express new ideas, technologies, and inventions, like astronauts and space shuttles. The Chickasaw Language Committee is a group of fluent Chickasaw speakers that meet regularly to create new Chickasaw words. Because Chickasaw is such a descriptive language, the committee works to preserve the richness and detail that is often lost in literal, word-for-word translations.

ENGLISH	CHICKASAW	PRONUNCIATION	DESCRIPTION
Astronaut	aba' nowa'	ah-bah' no-wa'	"above walker"
Blast off	tokafat aya	to-kah-faht ai-yah	"exploding it goes"
Boy	chipota nakni'	chi-poh-ta nug-ne'	"boy"
Dad	anki'	ang-ke'	"my dad"
Dance	hilha'	he-thlah'	"dance"
Eagle Feather	osi' hishi'	ohn-se' he-she'	"eagle feather"
Earth	yaakni'	yahk-nee'	"earth"
Float	okpalali	ok-pu-lah-lee	"float"
Flute	oskola'	os-koh-lah'	"flute"
Fly	wakaa	wah-kah	"fly"
Gravity	yaakni' aayokli'	yaakni' aayokli'	"holds it at the ground"
Helmet	yaalhipa kallo'	yah-thlee-pah kal-lo'	"a hard hat"

ENGLISH	CHICKASAW	PRONUNCIATION	DESCRIPTION
Mission	imaalammi	im-ah-lam-me	"mission"
Moon	oklhili hashi'	ok-thli-lee ha-she'	"night sun"
Pool	aayopi'	ah-yo-pee	"a place for swimming"
Sing	taloowa	tah-low-wa	"sing"
Outer Space	aba' pilla	a-bah' pil-lah	"way up there"
Space Shuttle	piini' wakaa'	pee-nee' wah-kah'	"flying canoe"
Space Station	aba' pilla aa-áyya'sha'	a-bah' pil-lah ai-yah'-sha'	"the place in outer-space where they live"
Spacesuit	aba' nowa' inaafka	a-bah' no-wa' ehn-naaf-kah	"above-walker clothes"
Spacewalk	aba' pilla nowa'	a-bah' pil-lah no-wa'	"outer-space walk"
Star	fochik	fo-chik	"star"
Sun	hashi'	ha-she'	"sun"
Rocket	naki' tokafa'	nu-ke' to-kah-fah'	"exploding arrow"

Ten..Nine..Eight..Seven..Six..Five..Four..Three..Two..One...BLAST OFF!

Pókko'li..Chakká'li..Ontochchi'na..Ontoklo..Hánna'li..
Talhlhá'pi..Oshta..Tochchi'na..Toklo..Chaffa...TOKAFAT AYA!